Do you know who you are?
xx Mommy
E
MELODI
ME
DERRICK

For my mom: Carolyn, my papa: Lovell, my sister: Sharvell, and my nephew: Damoni. My gratitude goes to you. Thank you for loving me endlessly and unconditionally. - L.L.B

For my mom. Thank you for believing in my dreams and always supporting me. Love You. - M.D

Missick Publishing Company LLCC
Missickpublishingcompany@gmail.com
Chicago, IL

LB: @lavellballard
MD: @maddymaakt

The art of this book was created digitally.

Be good, Be kind, LOVE *yourself*

Written by **Lavell Ballard**
Illustrations by **Madelon Davelaar**

It was almost bedtime. Elena decided to get ready for school tomorrow.

She wants to look her best.
But finding the perfect outfit
is difficult.

Elena's mom can't believe her eyes when she walks into the room.

"Baby, what is going on in here?"

"Mom, I don't want to get
ready for school tomorrow,"
said Elena.

"**Be good** to yourself,
school helps you grow,"
Mom said.

This was Elena's first week of school. Tomorrow is Friday. The last day of the week. On Fridays, you can wear whatever you would like. Elena wants to impress her classmates with her dream outfit.

"Mom, I want to be perfect for my classmates! Can I wear a princess outfit to school?"

Mom responded, "You can impress them just by being yourself.

Be kind to yourself, you are already perfect to me."

This was not going the way Elena wanted. She really wanted to wear her princess dress. She wanted to show her new friends. She also wanted to make more friends.

Maybe she could win them over with her hairstyle! Elena hands mom the flat iron, and other hair products.

"Mom, I want my hair to be just like my best friend Melody from school!"

Mom responds, "Maybe another time Elena. **Love yourself** the way I love you. Come on, let's go to the living room to do your hair."

Elena thought about what mom said to her: **Be good, Be kind, Love yourself**. Elena did not understand what mom meant. She only wanted to be stunning for her classmates. Instead she followed her mom into the living room.

Girls
ROCK

Elena loved when her mom counted while brushing her hair which helped her calm down. Together they sing:

1 - 2 - 3	Come on count with me
4 - 5 - 6	Shake your hips
7 - 8 - 9	Hands up
10	Let's do it again!

Mom also sang the naming game with her.

Sometimes we see things differently from how others may see them. We can find beauty in anything. You are extraordinary just like the items you love.

“What do you see, Elena?
asked Mom.
Elena shouted and pointed,
“A flower!”
“And that flower is as...?”
“...as beautiful as me!”
answered Elena.

Mom asked, “ I see a teddy bear,
Elena. What do you see?”
“I see a teddy bear as loving as me,”
said Elena.

They would play this game until Elena finished getting her hair braided.

"All done!" said Mom.

"How about you take a look?"

Elena loved her hair. The braids, beads, and bows. Everything was beautiful!

"You see it now baby?" Mom asked.

"You may not have the same hair as your classmates. You may not have the same shoes as your classmates. And you may not have the perfect clothes."

"But beauty is what YOU make it. You are your own kind of beautiful and that is what makes you powerful."

"Do you know who you are? You are the epitome of beauty. And the best thing about you is your heart."

Mom repeated, "**Be good** to yourself, **Be kind** to yourself, **Love yourself**!"

The first days Elena played with her classmates in the different area's.

She was very happy her classroom had. . .

. . .a block area. ..

. . .an art area. . .

. . .and a science area. She enjoys playing in each area. Throughout the week she would go to each area and learn something new.

KNOWLEDGE
Aa Bb Cc Dd Ee
Ff Gg Hh Ii Jj Kk
Ll Mm Nn Oo Pp
Qq Rr Ss Tt Uu

When Elena arrives at school, she peeks inside the classroom and starts to feel a little anxious. She really wishes she could have worn her princess outfit. But she realized that everyone had on their normal clothes. And everyone was different! Some friends had ponytails, locs, blonde hair, straight hair, and short hair.

She was not so afraid anymore!

Elena walks toward her friend Melody with confidence!

“Hi Melody. Would you like to play with me?”

Melody greets her enthusiastically, “Hi Elena. Yes, let’s play! Do you want to play dress-up? “

“Yes, to the house area we go!”

The girls try on many costumes.

Police officer

Construction worker

Chef

Doctors

Melody finally found a costume she thought was perfect. She snatched it quickly and put it on with excitement.

"I want to be perfect like Barbie when I grow up," Melody said. "She has everything. A crown, a princess gown and long pretty hair."

"**Be good** to yourself Melody. I think you are perfect the way tha you are," Elena said.

Their friend Derick runs up with excitement.

"Hi, Elena! Hi Melody! Can I play with you? Do you want to go to the block area?"

They excitedly agree.

Melody insists that they have a race with the toy cars.

"The one that makes it to the finish line first, is the fastest and the winner of the race."

Melody, who was so determined to win, decided to start the race.

"On your mark, get set,

GO!

“I’m winning, I'm winning!” yelled Derrick excited as he speeded to the play area.

“I won!”

Melody pouted, “No fair! Why can’t I be as fast as Derrick?”

Elena responded to Melody, "**Be kind** to yourself. What matters is that we all finished the race. You are a champion just like me. Maybe next time you can be the winner. For now, let's cheer for Derrick."

"Why can't I be
as good as
everyone else?
Why can't I win
like Derrick?
Why can't I have
beautiful hair
like Barbie?"

"My mom told me to be kind to myself, maybe you could too?" Elena suggested.

"But, I don't know how to be kind to myself.
I just want to
SCREEEEEEAAAMMMM. . ."

Elena thought back to what helped her calm down.

"When I'm upset, my mom and I count and sing," Elena said. "Why don't we do that too?"

1 - 2 - 3

Come on count with me

4 - 5 - 6

Shake your hips

7 - 8 - 9

Hands up

10

Let's do it again!

Together they sing the counting song. And again. And again. Until Melody felt better and forgot that she was angry in the first place..

Elena also sang the naming game with Melody.

"I see a treasure," said Elena.

"Melody what do you see?"

"I see a doll!"

"You are supposed to say, I see a treasure as lucky as me. Let's try again."

"Like you?"

Elena laughed. "No, like me!"

Melody confused. "Treasure as lucky as you? Or me?"

"You say, treasure as lucky as me!" explained Elena. "Now you say it."

After many times of practicing. Elena and Melody finally got it right.

"I see a treasure," Elena said. "Melody, what do you see?"

"I see a treasure as lucky as me!" Melody happily shouted.

"I feel better. You're a good friend, Elena," said Melody.

"**Love yourself**, Melody. You are my friend because you are you. You are a winner and you are glamorous. I love who you are."

Derrick got bored with all the singing. “Can we go and play with the blocks now?”

They gather the blocks and start building.

“Look, Elena, We made the tallest, gigantic, monstrous building ever. This is our dream house,” said Melody.

"Aw man," Derrick said with a sad face. "My building is too short. Your building is better than mine. I am going to make one just like yours."

Melody and Elena looked at each other because they knew just what to say to cheer Derrick up.

“**Be good** to yourself

Be kind to yourself…”

They said to Derrick.

". . .and **love yourself**!"

Do you know who you are?
xx Mommy
E
MELODI
ME
DERRICK

Ingram Content Group UK Ltd.
Milton Keynes UK
UKHW050259090523
421438UK00003B/10

9798218093341